Introduction

Today, over half of the intake of conscripts into the Soviet Army are Russian by birth. If one adds to this number the White Russians (Belorussians) and Little Russians (Ukrainians), both of them separate races, then the Slav is by far the preponderant element in the armed forces, outnumbering by about three to one the host of other nationalities such as the European Finns, Lithuanians, Letts and Estonians, and the many score of Asian peoples. All Soviet citizens irrespective of race are liable for conscripted service, the only exceptions

being on ... ...tness or of political unre... .. a large number of the non-Russ... ...ll have little knowledge of the Russ... ...gue, and this has to be made good at the ou ...set of military service since all instruction and orders are given in Russian. Although national titles are sometimes used, often in conjunction with a battle honour, there are in effect no minority national formations in the Soviet Army since these have been heavily diluted with Russians and Ukrainians.

Military service, even in the Soviet Union, is a leveller and educator. The discharged soldier returns to his Siberian *taiga* or Ural fishery fluent in both the Russian tongue and in the commissars' political jargon. The process of Russianization, begun so long ago in the times of early Muscovy, continues apace, and the Soviet Army has much in common with the Imperial Army of the Tsars.

The Tsarist Heritage

Following the lead of the victorious Prussians, Imperial Russia abandoned in 1874 its large long-service standing army for which recruits were selected by lot for twenty-five years with the colours, in favour of general short-term conscription. Service was originally set at six years, but by 1914 it had been reduced to three years for infantry and artillery and four years for all other arms. Conscripted recruits came principally from the Slav nationals, Russians, Ukrainians, White Russians and Poles, but included also natives of the Baltic States and certain parts of the Lower Volga and Caucasia. Finns from the Duchy of Finland and the Asian and Siberian peoples, with a few exceptions, were not accepted for conscripted military service.

Cadets at a Tsarist military school, c. 1880. (From V. S. Littauer's *The Russian Hussar*; J. A. Allen, London 1966.)

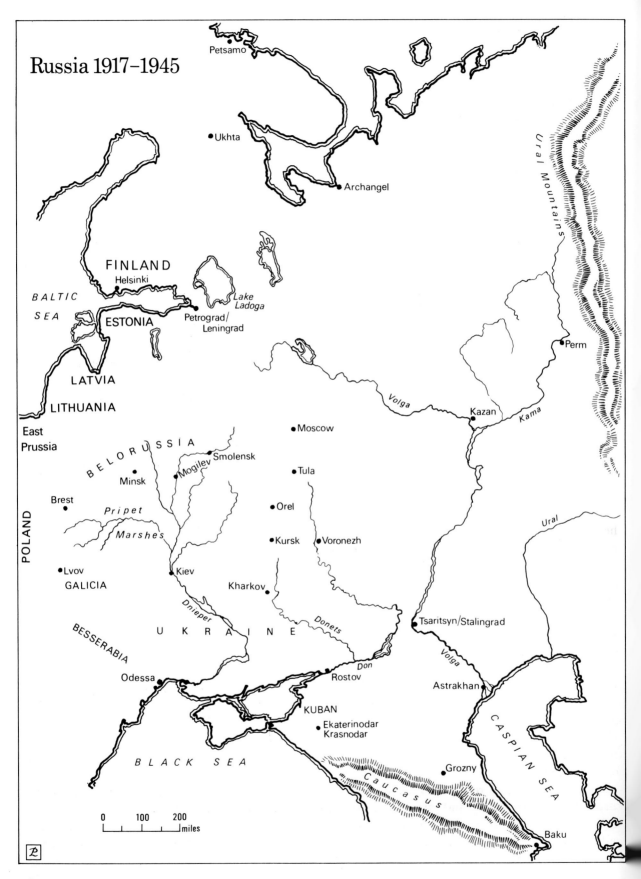

Russia 1917–1945

Petsamo

Ukhta

Archangel

Ural Mountains

FINLAND

Helsinki

BALTIC
SEA

Lake
Ladoga

ESTONIA

Petrograd/
Leningrad

Perm

LATVIA

Volga

Kazan

Kama

LITHUANIA

East
Prussia

Moscow

B E L O R U S S I A

Smolensk

Mogilev

Minsk

Tula

POLAND

Brest

Pripet

Orel

Ural

Marshes

Kursk

Voronezh

Lvov

Kiev

GALICIA

Kharkov

Dnieper

Tsaritsyn/Stalingrad

BESSERABIA

U K R A I N E

Donets

Don

Volga

Odessa

Rostov

Astrakhan

KUBAN

Ekaterinodar
Krasnodar

C A S P I A N

B L A C K   S E A

Caucasus

Grozny

S E A

0   100   200

└─┴─┴─┘ miles

Baku

The 1914 order of battle contained only a handful of minority national formations, a few brigades of Lettish and Finnish Rifles and some Turkestan and Caucasian cavalry and infantry divisions. The eleven divisions of Siberian Rifles consisted mostly of Russian settlers. The great majority of the formations which made up the Imperial Army were, in effect, Russian. Many Russian units, however, had a subsidiary recruiting area in a non-Russian (that is to say, Ukrainian or Polish) territory. And so two nationalities might be found in a single regiment, the non-Russian element being limited in size to thirty per cent of the total establishment. For political reasons neither the Russians nor the minority subject races were allowed to serve in their home areas.

Formerly the greater part of the officer corps came from the hereditary nobility and was linked with intellectual and ruling circles. The 1874 reforms, however, opened the officer's career to all classes, the qualification for entry being nationality, education and ability, so that the social origin of the Tsarist officer in the period from 1880 to 1914 became much more diverse. The guards and cavalry of the line continued, admittedly, to be officered by the wealthy, whether from noble, merchant or industrialist background, since the officer's pay in these regiments could cover only a small part of the necessary expenses. But officers of the main arms and technical corps came from the middle and lower middle classes and some were even of serf origin. Ninety per cent of infantry officers lived on their modest pay. As retirement ages were high, promotion was slow.

Whether of noble or plebeian origin, wealthy or poor, all officers had much in common, since long service in the *corps des pages* or the cadet and military *Junker* schools established a pattern even before commissioning. The strength of these regimental officers lay in their insight into the mentality of the Russian *muzhik* soldier, from whom by long and close proximity, or by birth, they were not far removed. As a class the professional regular officers were loyal to the Tsar.

Although the 1874 reforms made the officer corps more professional and created a strong trained reserve of other ranks which could be called back to the colours in time of war, they raised other difficulties and problems. The new officer society was very narrow in its outlook and was cut off from the court, the professions and political and intellectual circles, indeed from everyday life. The system of giving accelerated promotion to officers of the guard and general staff at the expense of the line officer, and of permitting over-age and inefficient chair-borne officers to remain in the service had a depressing effect on the junior and more energetic. Even fighting units were infected with the Russian bureaucracy of the times, so that officers became scribblers, spending hours every day on a multitude of inconsequential or unnecessary reports and returns. These deficiencies were brought to light during the heavy defeats in the Russo-Japanese War.

For this reason the military career was not popular and by 1910 the officer strength was more than 5,000 short of establishment. Since all officers served on long-service permanent commissions there was virtually no officer reserve. In time of war officer replacements had to be found by calling up ensigns of the reserve (*praporshchiki*), former junior non-commissioned officer conscripts with less than two years' service. The *praporshchik* had no training or experience as an officer but had earned an early discharge from the ranks merely by virtue of having completed secondary education and becoming so-called 'officer material'.

Another weakness of the short-term conscript army lay in the difficulty of recruiting a reliable and experienced corps of long-service non-commissioned officers. There was no permanent cadre and despite every encouragement it proved difficult to induce the conscript non-commissioned officers to prolong their service. In consequence the majority of the non-commissioned officers were found by promotion from the intake of conscripts.

From 1914 onwards casualties, particularly in the infantry, were very heavy among regimental officers and senior non-commissioned officers. Many of the replacement officers were *praporshchiki* or officer candidates from the intelligentsia, many with socialist revolutionary or egalitarian sympathies. Whereas the old type of regular officer, notwithstanding his many faults, was a simple soul who maintained his own rough and ready peasant discipline by fist or cudgel, his replacement hated military life and was too lazy or too lacking in character to enforce orders or look after the welfare

5

of the troops. And so after 1914 there rapidly grew a yawning gulf between officers and men.

Contemporary First World War sources have stressed that the Russian soldier required more leading and driving than any other soldier in Europe. Well led, he was formidable; without leaders of quality, he was of little account. The soldiers, naturally enough, had the faults and the virtues of their race. Centuries of Tartar domination and Muscovite serfdom had robbed them of initiative; they were lazy by nature and would do nothing unless put to it. On the other hand, as though in compensation, history and environment had left them hardy, stoical and with great endurance. They were subject to sudden changes of mood for which they themselves could not account; they could be stolid or mercurial, good-humoured or grim, peaceable or aggressive, heroic or cowardly, kindly and generous or unbelievably brutal and cruel.

Before 1914 one recruit out of four had no knowledge whatever of the Russian language. Of the Russian recruits four out of five could not read or write; all orders had to be read aloud to them.

By German standards the 1914 Tsarist Army was inadequately trained and indifferently led. And yet the Russian soldier was undoubtedly superior to any of the troops of the Austro-Hungarian Empire and the efficiency of the Tsarist High Command compared favourably with that of the Habsburgs. The most reliable and probably the most efficient troops of the Russian Army were the artillery and the cavalry, and these maintained their morale and discipline long after the other arms were in a state of dissolution. At the other end of the scale were the sappers and miners, recruited mainly from industrial workers, a corps with a long record of disorder and mutiny in the years between 1905 and 1914.

The Tsarist Army entered the First World War unprepared and poorly equipped. Sufficient munitions and supplies were never produced for the 15,500,000 men mobilized during the war; Imperial Russia had reserves of men but no rifles, horses but no saddles or sabres, and little ammunition for the guns available. Only six million rifles were manufactured against a requirement of seventeen million; Britain, Japan and the United States could not make good the deficiency in time.

Wave upon wave of Russian infantry attacked German positions with little or no artillery support, only to be driven back when just short of their objectives by the devastating weight of the defensive fire of the enemy.

The Revolution

By 1915 Russian losses had mounted to 2,300,000 and, at a secret ministerial meeting held early that summer, General Polivanov, the Minister for War, described the situation in the gloomiest terms, placing his hopes 'on the immeasurable distances, the impassable roads, the deep mud and the grace of St Nicolas'. The heavy losses had diluted and transformed both the commissioned and the non-commissioned officers' corps, and within the army a social revolution had already taken place. Yet the fate of the Romanovs was to depend not on the constancy of the army in the field but on the draft and training units and the rear installations in the area of the capital. These rear units had one over-riding motive, that of avoiding front-line service.

Tsar Nicolas II, the last of the Romanovs, had once more ignored the advice of his ministers when in September 1915 he had personally taken over the supreme command of the Russian forces and the field command in the West. The field command or *Stavka* was located not in Petrograd or Moscow but in the Belorussian city of Mogilev. In neither Mogilev nor Petrograd itself, was there a single trained and disciplined regiment with any experience of war, even of the Imperial Guard.

On 8 March 1917 there began in Petrograd a series of mass civil demonstrations, sparked off by a shortage of bread, protesting against the war, the government and the police. Socialist Revolutionary, Menshevik and anarchist agitators took advantage of the situation and the police were deliberately singled out for attack. The Cossacks, instead of supporting the civil authority, remained passive. On Monday 12 March a training draft of the Volinsky Life Guard Regiment killed its commander and, calling on men from the Preobrazhensky and Litovsky Guard Regiments to join it, mutinied. Petrograd was given over to anarchy and a few days later the Tsar abdicated.

The period between the first March Revolution and the Bolshevik November Revolution saw the desertion or self-disbandment of most of the old Imperial Army. The reins of administration had been taken up firstly by Lvov's Provisional Government and then by Kerensky's, although in truth both governments were accountable neither to themselves nor to the people but to the self-appointed Petrograd Soviet of Workers' and Soldiers' Deputies, one of the chairmen of which was Leon Trotsky. The many Soviets which sprang up all over the country would obey no order from the Provisional Government unless the Petrograd Soviet was in agreement. By the same token the armed forces owed their allegiance not to Kerensky but to the Petrograd Soviet.

At this stage the revolution was still bloodless but a heady spirit of liberalism was in the air. This quickly spread to the troops. By Military Order No. 1, published in *Izvestia*, the newspaper of the Petrograd Soviet, and by the 'Declaration of the Rights of Soldiers' which followed it, the armed forces were isolated from the parliamentary *Duma* and the *Stavka*, the control of military operations and warlike equipment being handed over to the soldiers' elected committees. Officers were not to be issued with arms, and troops were encouraged to refer complaints against officers to the soldiers' committees. Saluting and standing to attention outside duty hours was stopped, and the accepted modes of address such as 'Your Excellency' and 'Your Honour' when talking to higher-ranking officers were forbidden. The fanning of a mistrust of all officers as a reactionary class, and the removal of their authority over their men, equipment and arms, could lead only to the rapid disintegration of the Russian Army. A deep rift had already been driven between officers and the rank and file, and agitators were already urging, sometimes in the crudest and most violent terms, the replacement of officers by commanders elected from the ranks. Desertion was rife, the numbers running to millions.

If it had not been for the Bolshevik November Revolution and the Civil War which followed, it is probable that the old Russian Army would have entirely disappeared. It was owing to Trotsky that the remnants were salvaged and the process of disintegration and demoralization reversed. The new revolutionary Red Army owed its foundations to the Imperial Army of the Tsar; it was, as Lenin expressed it, 'built out of the bricks of the old'.

The Birth of the Red Army

When the Bolsheviks seized power in Petrograd, they relied neither on the bulk of the mutinous soldiery nor on the peasants. Instead they created a situation in which industry and government organs were paralysed and the armed forces were benevolently or apathetically passive. In the final outcome the *coup d'état* rested on a few armed detachments sympathetic to the Bolsheviks, usually foreign units such as the Lettish Rifles, some turbulent revolutionary naval detachments and a hard core of armed factory levies known as Red Guards.

Lenin's views on the establishing of regular armed forces within the communist state were by no means clear. At one time he appears to have favoured a part-time armed militia and was against a permanent standing army. Before the March Revolution and during the short-lived period of the Kerensky Government, his policy towards the military was in some respects parallel to that which he adopted towards industry. Lenin professed to believe that capitalism must be smashed, if necessary by anarchy, before it could

Members of the Red Army in Poland, 1920. (Hulton)

Typical Red Army 'military specialists', formerly Tsarist officers, Poland, 1920. (Hulton)

be replaced by his own brand of socialism. And so he appears to have given his support to the system of soldiers' committees, probably because it destroyed the authority of the military commanders and broke down discipline. Without a disciplined military there could be no counter-revolution.

Lenin could not fail to learn the lesson of Kerensky's grossest error, namely, that of his neglect to win the allegiance of a reliable and disciplined body of troops. No sooner had the Bolsheviks seized power than they formed their own secret police, the Cheka, together with its own subordinate military detachments usually made up of Latvians, Serbs, Chinese or other foreign mercenaries indifferent to Russian politics and largely impervious to White counter-propaganda. And so the caucus of the highly centralized police state was already in being.

Although Lenin professedly advocated pacifism when Kerensky was in office, the reality of power either revealed him in his true colours or forced upon him a complete change of front; for, having done his utmost to discredit and subvert the Imperial Army, Lenin was soon obliged to repair the damage and rebuild a regular armed force powerful enough to safeguard the new Bolshevik

régime against counter-revolution and the steady eastward advance of the troops of the Central Powers. For the Kronstadt and Helsinki bluejackets had been penetrated by anarchists and were not amenable to discipline, whether Tsarist or Bolshevik, and the Petrograd Red Guards, although said to number about 20,000 at this time, had only very limited military value.

At the time, the Bolshevik November *coup* had appeared to be the final straw in breaking up what remained of the Russian Army. Large numbers of officers, alarmed at the bitter class hatred preached by the Bolsheviks and their allies, made their way either as armed bodies of men or individually in disguise, to the south-east, to the territories of the traditionally conservative Don Cossacks, to form there the first of the White Armies. Yet many of the formations of the old Russian Army still in contact with the German or Austro-Hungarian enemy kept their organization and their cohesion in spite of their lowered efficiency and relatively poor morale. A proportion of the former officers still remained and these formations, providing part of what was known as the Western screens, were to form the core of the new Red Army. Elsewhere many former Tsarist officers, particularly those in the Ministries and the larger headquarters, passed into the Bolshevik command organization without a break in their service. In this way part of the heritage of the old army was transferred to the new.

Yet the new Red Army was not formally brought into existence until the official decree of January 1918, nor was there any clear pattern in its establishment. Side by side with the regular field formations providing the bulk of the screens, there was a mass induction of Red Guard members by the voluntary recruitment of industrial workers on an extendable three months' engagement at a fixed rate of pay of 150 roubles a month. Although numbers of these must have included idealist party-workers, the majority came from the unemployed, anxious to get a meal ticket, together with a criminal minority. Elsewhere, outside Moscow and Petrograd, local soviets raised and paid their own military formations and detachments, recruiting them either from industrial workers or from former military units. The methods of command and administration varied

Red Army cavalry in Moscow, 1921. (Hulton)

from place to place and the commanders were either elected or appointed arbitrarily by local committees. Many of the new military commanders were Red Guard Bolsheviks or soldiers from the rank and file.

Lenin was forced to come to terms with the Central Powers at the Peace of Brest Litovsk, signed in March 1918. This lost the Bolsheviks the whole of the Ukraine and part of South-East Russia in the area of Rostov-on-Don. General Kornilov's White Volunteer Army, the rank and file of which was made up largely of former officers, had begun to overrun the Kuban and the Caucasus. Finland, Poland and the Baltic States had already seceded from Russia and a counter-revolutionary movement in Siberia under Admiral Kolchak, aided by a Czecho-Slovak corps recruited from former prisoners of war, began to move steadily westwards along the axis of the Trans-Siberian railway. Japanese troops

were already in Vladivostok, and Britain, France and the United States, in an effort to bring Russia back into the war against Germany, began to ship material and military aid to the Whites in Odessa, the Caucasus, Siberia, Archangel and the Baltic States. The German military occupation authorities in the Ukraine, despite the fact that the Empire was now at peace with the new Soviet State, gave arms and moral support to their eastern neighbour, General Krasnov, the *Ataman* of the Don Cossacks, in his struggle to maintain his newly-found independence from Russia.

During the summer and early autumn of 1918 it looked as if the new Soviet régime would be extinguished. The majority, some of them probably the best, of the officers of the old Russian Army had either been driven out, often into the arms of the Whites, or murdered. Although the Reds were vastly superior to the Whites in numbers of men and material, their discipline and

9

A Red Army parade in Rostov-on-Don in 1920. (Novosti Press Agency)

leadership were poor; command by committee and revolutionary fervour were not enough.

Lenin and Trotsky, however, were hard-headed realists. The naval officer staffs who first came into contact with Lenin as early as December 1917 were surprised at his insistence on restoring discipline; the unquestioning acceptance of centralized authority had always been Lenin's *credo*. In March 1918 Trotsky, the brilliant and impetuous Ukrainian Jew, had left his post as Commissar for Foreign Affairs to become Commissar for War. Equipping himself with an armoured train hauled by two locomotives and provided with a radio centre, a library and military headquarters, automobiles and a large military escort, he set off on his lightning tours of the various fronts, rarely at rest, covering thousands of miles in his travels.

Lenin had no clear military policy except in his insistence on a military discipline which was eventually to prove even more exacting than the Bolshevik political discipline. He would not admit defeat and was prepared to pay a ruthless price for success in the lives of others, though the cost might be reckoned in millions. Yet, despite his lack of military experience, he closely followed the day-to-day conduct of the Civil War, threatening, chiding, often directly interfering with the details of the high command. Trotsky, on the other hand, originally no better informed than Lenin in military matters, was closer to the military staffs and the actual conduct of operations in the field, and thus soon amassed a fund of knowledge and acquired a certain expertise and flair for strategy and for military training and organization. Ruthless, vain and unfeeling, he was nevertheless a highly educated or at least a quick-witted man, and had the knack of getting on with the former officer staffs still in Red Army service, whose abilities he used to the full.

Both Lenin and Trotsky were of one mind in suppressing all command by committee. They soon sent the elected commanders packing. But Trotsky went even further. He had little faith in territorial or part-time soldiers or in partisan or guerrilla bands as a substitute for a permanent regular army. Repeated defeats in the field convinced him that the new Red Army would not win through to victory without the aid of professional officers and of non-commissioned officers. He won Lenin's reluctant support and on 29 May 1918 a resolution was agreed by the All-Russian Executive Committee changing the voluntary recruitment of the armed forces to one of enforced mobilization of workers and poor peasants. Former officers and non-commissioned officers of the old army, although hardly within this mobilization category, were subjected to compulsory call-up and, before the following November, 23,000 former officers and officials, including military doctors, veterinary surgeons and paymasters, and 110,000 former non-commissioned officers already formed part of the new Red Army.

Trotsky, like Stalin, had a marked ability to make good use of the instrument left by his predecessors and adapt it to his own needs. Although he has been given the credit for introducing into the Red Army the system of political commissars, what he did was to continue and extend the innovations already introduced by Kerensky. Kerensky had been so antagonistic to and suspicious of the military that he had introduced into the armed forces political commissars to act as watchdogs on the generals and to serve as intermediaries between the commanders and the soldiers' committees. Other communist-appointed commissars were to be found in the Collegium for the Organization of the Red Army in Petrograd as early as December 1917.

Under Trotsky the appointment of all political commissars was regulated from the centre and their role was to protect the new régime from counter-revolution by keeping a check on the reliability of the commanders. In this way the commissar became the military commander's shadow and exercised what was in effect a dual command in that no military order of any consequence was valid unless it bore his countersignature. At first, commissars were appointed down to the level of divisions but eventually, before the end of the Civil War, they were to be

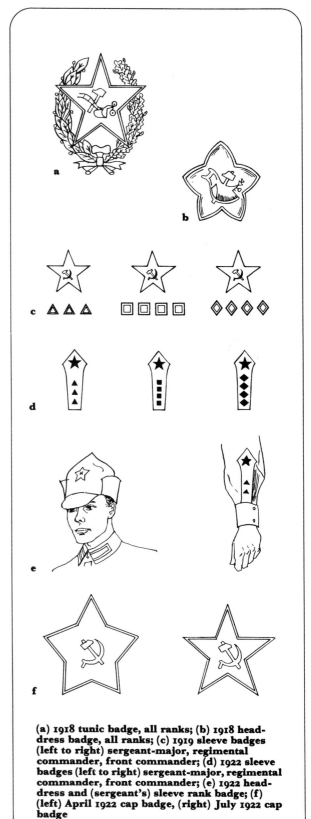

(a) 1918 tunic badge, all ranks; (b) 1918 head-dress badge, all ranks; (c) 1919 sleeve badges (left to right) sergeant-major, regimental commander, front commander; (d) 1922 sleeve badges (left to right) sergeant-major, regimental commander, front commander; (e) 1922 head-dress and (sergeant's) sleeve rank badge; (f) (left) April 1922 cap badge, (right) July 1922 cap badge

found in all major units. This commissar system, although originally intended as a temporary political counterweight to the re-employed military officer, was permanently retained as part of the organization of both the Red Army and the Soviet Army.

The early commissar was not necessarily a communist party member. More often than not he was an applicant considered suitable for the job simply on the strength of his proletarian background and Bolshevik sympathies. His degree of military experience was of secondary importance, and many of the original appointments were filled by ruffians in quest of power or loot. But, as Trotsky's fanatical and ruthless grip took increasing hold, not even the commissars were safe, and numbers were shot for the failure of their troops. Thus there came into being a new race of army political workers, callous, ambitious party members, full of tireless energy, driven on by fear of failure and dread of consequent denunciation.

The commissar, then as now, was also responsible 'for the cultural enlightenment and the political, as well as the general, education of the troops'. He was expected to be the best informed man in his formation or unit. He could never hope to have close ties with his subordinates and with the men themselves, without the presence in the ranks of communist agitators, party members whose task it was to talk with the troops hour by hour and day by day, on parade ground or in the barrack room, spreading the directed line of propaganda and carefully noting each soldier's reactions and views. Since the communist soldier was trained as an agitator-spy, all information picked up was carefully retailed to the commissar.

In 1918, however, Trotsky's insistence on close control from the centre was bitterly opposed by many of the regional soviets, some of whom were scandalized by his use of 'the Tsar's flunkeys', the former officers. Most of these had come back to the army unwillingly, many of them only awaiting the opportunity to desert to the Whites. But the alternative to service was death or incarceration in a concentration camp, and their families were already held hostage for their loyalty. Trotsky seems to have treated the former officers on his staff, superficially at least, with tact and to have

made good use of their talents; but elsewhere the re-employed officer, particularly if returning to command or regimental appointments in the field, was met with hostility and resentment alike from the elected soldier or party man whom he displaced and from the rank and file who regarded him with suspicion as a bar to their own advancement. The commissar with whom the former officer was obliged to work most closely was in all probability the same agitator who had done his utmost to destroy the old Tsarist Army, one of the Bolsheviks who were believed by many officers to be in the pay of the Germans. Among the rank and file even the word 'officer' was anathema, so that the re-employed and rankless officers became known as 'military specialists' or 'red commanders'.

The Civil War

The first threat to the new Bolshevik régime came in May 1918 from South-East Russia and the Caucasus. The rich, industrial, grain- and coal-producing area of the Ukraine had been lost to Russia by the signing of the treaty of Brest Litovsk, and the Politburo, now housed in the new capital of Moscow, was forced to rely on the corn from the rich farming areas of the North Caucasus. General Kornilov's White Volunteer Army, though only 5,000 strong, had already begun the conquest of the Kuban. Further to the north Krasnov's Don Cossacks had ended their long flirtation with Moscow and were beginning to press northward into the Voronezh *guberniya* (province) and eastward towards the Lower Volga in order to round off the Don Cossack territories which, they fondly imagined, would remain an autonomous region independent of Russia.

The Volunteer Army had already broken the railway from Rostov and Tsaritsyn (later Stalingrad) to Novorossisk on the Black Sea, and the movement of the Don Cossacks towards the Lower Volga threatened to cut the rail and river communications between the North Caucasus and the capital. Both Moscow and Petrograd were already on very scant rations and were virtually without reserves of food.

A 1920 standard bearers' party of Budenny's 1 Cavalry Army. (Novosti Press Agency)

At the beginning of June, Stalin, a comparatively little-known member of the Politburo, was sent to Tsaritsyn to organize the food supplies from the North Caucasus. From there he was to proceed to Novorossisk. Circumstances kept him at Tsaritsyn where, at his own insistence, he was made the principal political commissar to both 10 Army, which was holding the Tsaritsyn area, and the North Caucasus Front, the headquarters of which was based on the same city. Virtually dismissing General Snesarev, a former Cossack officer commanding the North Caucasus Front, together with his commissar, Stalin was for several months the *de facto* front commander, although his command was so scattered and his communications so uncertain that his control did not extend far beyond the territorial limits of 10 Army.

In Tsaritsyn Stalin became closely acquainted with a number of military commanders whom he subsequently selected for the highest ranks in the Red Army; these included Voroshilov, the Commander of 10 Army, an old Bolshevik without military experience, Shchadenko, the commissar, and Budenny, a cavalry sergeant-major who was second-in-command of 1 (Socialist) Cavalry Regiment. Motivated by ambition and jealousy, Stalin secretly supported and intrigued with what was to become known as Voroshilov's Tsaritsyn opposition to Trotsky's reforms and organizational methods. Trotsky's use of the former officer specialists was a measure which came under special attack, Stalin taking it upon himself to have the Cheka secret police arrest the officers as they arrived from Moscow. This widened the rift, not merely between Stalin and Trotsky, but more particularly between Stalin and those senior Red Army officers who were of the Trotsky school. When Stalin eventually came to power, nearly all of them paid the extreme penalty.

Although many years later Voroshilov, when Stalin's Commissar for Defence, extolled Stalin's military ability and the part played by the Tsaritsyn defenders during the Civil War, in reality the only threat to the revolution in the area of the

Lower Volga came from the probes of the Don Cossack cavalry. In one of these thrusts General Mamontov actually penetrated to the outskirts of the city. But the Cossacks had always lacked staying power and they disliked being separated from their own territories and the support of infantry. Their discipline was too loose and their mounted training somewhat too specialized to turn them into regular fighting men.

Stalin's main contribution to the fighting was probably in supply, transport and equipment matters, for which he had some ability, and in the repressive police measures which, together with his Cheka colleague Dzerzhinsky, he took against both the military and the civil organizations.

Much more bitter fighting took place further to the south in the Kuban and the Caucasus where the White Volunteer Army, since Kornilov's death under the command of Denikin, together with the Kuban Cossacks waged a bloody war against Red Guards and irregulars, estimated to have a strength of 100,000–200,000 men. There Russian committed against Russian, brother against brother, father against son, every kind of brutal and bestial atrocity. Whole populations of towns and villages were often butchered.

Further to the north in Siberia, Admiral Kolchak relied heavily on the support given him by the disciplined and trained Czecho-Slovak corps, but his relationship with the Czech commanders was bedevilled by politics, intrigue and petty jealousies. By the end of 1918 he had become dictator in the east, and had raised large White Russian forces by the conscription of former officers and other ranks back into the service. At first he achieved some striking successes, taking the great city of Perm, 700 miles east of Moscow, on Christmas Day; it appeared that he might join up with the counter-revolutionary forces near Archangel. But Kolchak was to fail because he lacked the determination and cold-blooded ruthlessness of his Red opponents and had no experience of handling troops in the field. His choice of subordinates was unfortunate and, even with sufficient armament and stores at his disposal, he was unable to overcome the problems of administration, movement and supply. His troops went hungry and unsupported.

Moreover, like the other White generals,

Kolchak lacked popular appeal. To the Russian peasant and worker he represented the old discredited order of Tsardom. The Bolsheviks, on the other hand, enjoyed some popularity, even though limited and short-lived, among the workers and peasants because of their golden promises of redistributed land and workers' participation in the profits of industry. Even the non-Russian minorities had been promised autonomy.

But the population was for the most part tired and apathetic, and heartily sick of shortages and war. With the exception of the fanatical communists and the die-hard officer loyalists, men had to be dragooned into both the Red and the White services, and the figures for desertions on both sides ran into millions. Sometimes the men took to the woods and became bandits; but more usually they simply threw their weapons away and made off home. Both sides came to realize that prisoners, rather than being put to death or kept in captivity, could more profitably be offered the choice of death or enlistment with their captors. Their new recruits, however, were usually unreliable material; units frequently changed sides taking their arms with them, and then, liking their new conditions of service no better than the old, changed back again. Yet even in this problem of loyalty the Reds had an advantage over the Whites in that the communists were better fitted, both by mentality and training and by their party and Cheka police organization, to keep a closer check on their military subordinates and a more repressive hand on their troops.

Numbers of Red commanders distinguished themselves in the fighting against Kolchak on the eastern front. Stalin was there on the northern flank for about three weeks after the fall of Perm, but his role was restricted to that for which he was suited, a Cheka purge of unsuccessful and unlucky military commanders and civil functionaries. Frunze, an old Bolshevik and revolutionary assassin and later Commissar for War, commanded the right flank with some success. But the predominant role was played by Trotsky and his two principal military advisers, firstly Vatsetis, a Lettish color of the old Imperial Army, and then S. S. Kamenev, a former colonel of the General Staff who was the military specialist commander

Trotsky, Kalinin, Frunze, Budenny and Clara Zetkin on the stand in Red Square during the celebrations of the 7th Anniversary of the Bolshevik Revolution. (Hulton)

of the east front and later, after July 1918, the titular Red Army Commander-in-Chief.

With the withdrawal of the Czechs, Kolchak's forces began slowly to disintegrate, and in the following year he himself was caught and shot by the Reds.

The next heavy blow made against the Bolsheviks came from the Baltic shore where a former Imperial general by the name of Yudenich, with Estonian military and financial support, collected a White Russian force hardly stronger than an army corps and in the autumn of 1919 advanced eastward towards Narva and Petrograd. His success was immediate and within weeks White cavalry had reached the outskirts of the former capital. Trotsky was sent by the Politburo to organize the Red defences, and reinforcements were rushed by rail from the Moscow area.

At the time, the world confidently expected Petrograd to fall within a matter of days. But Yudenich failed in his mission for two simple reasons. Firstly, a subordinate neglected to cut the Petrograd–Moscow railway along which Red troop trains were racing into the city; and secondly, because Yudenich's communications were broken by the demolition of viaducts, and he was unable to overcome the well-nigh insuperable problem of supplying his own troops. With the onset of winter his men were near starvation and a

few weeks later his troops fell back rapidly into Estonia.

The efforts of the White generals had hitherto been largely unco-ordinated, succeeding one another rather than concerted. The first campaign had been the operations of Kornilov's and Denikin's Volunteer Army in the far-away Kuban and Caucasus and Krasnov's thrusts on the Lower Volga. Then had followed Kolchak's movement westward towards Moscow. Only when Kolchak was in retreat in the east did Yudenich attack from the north-west. Yet Yudenich's offensive *was* mounted at the same time as that of Denikin from the south.

It was at the time of Yudenich's thrust on Petrograd that the Soviet State appeared to be in danger of obliteration. Denikin, no longer the Commander of the Volunteer Army but now the Commander-in-Chief in South Russia, controlled Mai-Maevsky's Volunteer Army, Sidorin's Don Cossacks and Wrangel's Caucasian Army. Denikin had begun to advance in May 1919 from the Caucasus and the Don Cossack territory to the north of Rostov into Central Russia and the Ukraine. For the Ukraine had been reoccupied by the Reds after the withdrawal of the Austro-German troops in the previous November, and was torn by warring factions and armed banditry.

Denikin was fighting against odds; he was

greatly outnumbered by Bolshevik troops and had been unable to bring the Poles in on his side. He was, however, relatively well provided with British equipment and he numbered among his commanders the best leaders in any of the Russian armies, Red or White. His failure was one not of resources or of supply, but of strategy. His principal and probably correct aim was to take Moscow. But he dispersed his troops in a great 180-degrees arc, ordered them on to objectives as far apart as Odessa and Kiev to the west and Tsaritsyn and Saratov to the east. His subsequent success was admittedly remarkable in that by October of that year, very much at about the same time as Yudenich was nearing Petrograd, White troops had overrun almost the whole of the Ukraine and had moved into Central Russia, taking Kursk, Voronezh and Orel, little more than 200 miles from the capital; in the east, Sidorin and Wrangel had taken Tsaritsyn and were on the road to Saratov. The troops of the Bolshevik South Front had simply melted away.

But Denikin's command had already been fatally over-extended and dispersed and now covered a frontage of about 1,600 miles. Winter was approaching and the presence of bandits, partisans and armed Ukrainian nationalists made the areas to his rear insecure.

The Soviet military commander of the South Front, a former officer by name of Gittis, was replaced firstly by Egorev and then, some weeks later, by Egorov. Stalin was transferred from the West to the South Front as political commissar where he was joined temporarily by Trotsky. From about this time dated the bitter controversy as to whether Denikin should be counter-attacked from the area of the Lower Volga in the east or from the north in the area of Voronezh and thence southward down the Donets Basin. The latter course proved the successful one and the credit for it was claimed by both Trotsky and Stalin.

Much of Denikin's success had been due to his use of raiding cavalry columns under the Cossack generals Mamontov and Shkuro, deep in the Red Army rear. Budenny's cavalry corps, reorganized as 1 Cavalry Army, was transferred from the Volga to the area of Voronezh in order to engage the White raiders. The Reds took their tactics from the pattern of the Whites and penetrated between the Volunteer Army and the Don Cossacks. By the end of October 1919, 1 Cavalry Army, which included in its columns the future cavalry leaders Timoshenko and Zhukov, had taken Voronezh and was moving rapidly southward towards Rostov-on-Don, hoping to envelop Sidorin and Wrangel in the Don bend and on the Lower Volga between Tsaritsyn and Astrakhan. To escape being cut off, Denikin began his long retreat to the Crimea and the North Caucasus; amid cruel scenes of violence and disorder the Whites were driven out of the Caucasus, but held on temporarily to the area of the Crimea. Denikin gave up his command to Wrangel. The last of the Whites were now doomed.

The Russo-Polish War

In 1914 Poland had long been partitioned between Germany, Austro-Hungary and Russia, Eastern Poland being a province of the Russian Empire. Following the Russian Revolution and the collapse of the Central Powers, the new Polish Republic had come into being.

A fervently nationalist Poland, bitterly anti-Russian rather than anti-Bolshevik, had no wish to see a strong Russia on its eastern frontier since it regarded this as a threat to its own existence. Piłsudski, Poland's leader, trusted Denikin as little as he did Lenin, and in 1919 he had ignored Denikin's overtures for a joint Russo-Polish campaign against the Bolsheviks. Meanwhile, however, he was, through intermediaries, in secret correspondence with Trotsky. Piłsudski took no notice of Moscow's efforts to secure an armistice; he did not want peace. Nor, for the moment, did he want war; so he contented himself with awaiting the outcome of the Red/White struggle. In the long term he hoped to secure for Poland the White Russian and Ukrainian territories once held by the powerful eighteenth-century Kingdom of Poland. At the same time, he probably hoped to detach from Russia the remainder of the Ukraine and Caucasia, and make them into puppet states dependent for their existence on an alliance with Poland.

Meanwhile skirmishing and border fighting

continued between the Poles and the Red Army and by 1919 Polish troops had already established themselves in Belorussia and Galicia as far east as Vilna, Minsk and Lwów.

In April 1920, 3 Polish Army suddenly attacked in great strength into the Ukraine. Advancing rapidly eastward, it reached the Dnieper and seized Kiev, the capital, in the first week in May. The invasion caused a wave of indignation and national fervour among the Russian people and large numbers of volunteers, irrespective of class or political belief, offered their services to the Red Army. Once more there was a frantic reorganization of the Soviet High Command. Troops already deployed against Wrangel were withdrawn from the South Ukraine. Gittis was removed from the command of the West Front, making way for a former lieutenant of the Imperial Guards named Tukhachevsky, an ambitious and energetic young officer, commissioned only in 1914, who had spent three years in German captivity before returning to Russia and joining the Bolshevik Party. Stalin, as political commissar, rejoined the old south front, now redesignated the South-West Front, and still under the leadership of the military specialist Egorov. Budenny's 1 Cavalry Army, with Voroshilov as its political commissar, was ordered back from the Caucasus to the area of the middle Dnieper, arriving there at the end of May.

Egorov's initial successes were due in no small part to the mobility of 1 Cavalry Army. Although this force numbered little more than 16,000 men it was boldly handled by Budenny; some success was due also to Timoshenko's 6 Cavalry Division. By the second week in June the cavalry, together with 12 Soviet Army, had started to outflank the enemy and it looked as if 3 Polish Army would be surrounded in the area of Kiev. The Poles fell back quickly, however, to escape the encirclement and Egorov's South-West Front took up the pursuit westwards into Galicia.

Tukhachevsky was originally separated from Egorov by the almost impenetrable belt of the Pripet Marshes, running nearly 300 miles from west to east and 150 miles from north to south. But the marshland gave way to firm and open country as the two Soviet fronts entered Poland. Tukhachevsky, with a force of over 100,000 men, com-

Frunze, the Commissar for War, at a 1925 inspection. (Novosti Press Agency)

prising four armies and a cavalry corps, had already begun his own offensive in the north in the first week in July. The Poles were in full retreat. Vilna, Minsk and Brest Litovsk were taken, and the West Front began to close on Warsaw. It appeared as if Poland itself were about to be overrun.

Yet the Red Army, standing on the threshold of victory, was decisively defeated. As many contemporary photographs show, a large proportion of the Soviet fighting men were little more than civilians hurriedly equipped with rifles. Units were apt to disintegrate at the first serious check, and there was a very high rate of desertion. Overmuch reliance had been placed on the revolutionary spirit of the Polish proletariat, but these, instead of going over to the Reds, resisted the Bolsheviks with all their might, fighting, sometimes in the Soviet rear, with shot-guns and hunting rifles. A French military mission had already arrived in Warsaw to assist the Polish High Command, and when the Poles counter-attacked, the Red Army troops began to give way.

Tukhachevsky had hardly three years' military experience of any sort and his deployment followed some half-learned school copy-book theme. His troops stood on the Vistula immediately east of the Polish capital and he had successfully contrived to envelop Warsaw from the north and north-west by extending forward his right shoulder. On this flank also he had deployed Gai's cavalry corps. But he had no uncommitted reserve and his own left flank, which had formerly enjoyed the protection of the Pripet Marshes, was open and vulnerable.

S. S. Kamenev, the military specialist Commander-in-Chief, in a directive issued in the first week in August, was said to have ordered Tukhachevsky's West Front on to Warsaw. Egorov's South-West Front was ordered to move troops north-westward to close on Tukhachevsky's exposed left flank. It was later argued that Kamenev's directive to the South-West Front ordering 1 Cavalry Army and 12 Army away from Lwów and on to Warsaw was not clear. This may have been so. Certain it is that Stalin, Budenny and Voroshilov deliberately chose to misunderstand it, for even as late as the third week in August they were still resisting any orders which moved the cavalry army away from the Lwów axis. When they did move it was already too late. The Poles had enveloped Tukhachevsky's open southern flank and began to roll up the West Front from south to north. Hemmed in to the north by German East Prussian territory, the Red Army men either passed over the frontier to be interned *en masse* or took to their heels eastward in an attempt to escape the encircling pincer. By September all the Russian forces were in retreat and the Poles, following up, reoccupied most of Belorussia and Galicia.

Hostilities ended with the signing of the Treaty of Riga in October 1920. The Red Army had come out of the Polish War with little credit and its relatively poor showing was one of the factors which caused it to be much underestimated in Western Europe in the period between the two World Wars.

The End of the Civil War

While the Russo-Polish War was being fought, Wrangel had attempted to take advantage of the situation by breaking out of the Crimea back into the former territories of the Don and Kuban Cossacks. At first he had some success but, after the signing of the Treaty of Riga, Red Army troops began to arrive from the western theatre. The South Front, commanded by Frunze, began a late October counter-offensive which drove the Whites back into the Crimean Peninsula. During November 1920 a final offensive was made into the Crimea across the shallow salt marshes of the Lazy Sea and the remnants of Wrangel's force were destroyed. Only the fortunate escaped with their families by ship from the terrible vengeance of the commissar and the Cheka.

A few months later Blukher, one of the successful Red commanders in the Crimea, undertook the reduction of the last counter-revolutionary force in the Far East Maritime Provinces where the White General Semenov, a brigand and puppet of the Japanese, held the railway between Khabarovsk and Vladivostok. It was not, however, until the end of 1922, after the evacuation of the Japanese, that Semenov's forces were finally driven over the border into Manchuria.

An Army without confidence

The Red Army at the end of the Civil War was a mass of partially trained, poorly equipped and ill-disciplined conscripts whose only wish was to go home. Its muster rolls numbered several million, but the desertion rate was very high and the bureaucratic army system so inefficient and cumbersome that the order of battle never totalled more than about seventy divisions. Many of these formations were divisions only in name, having strengths no greater than those of the establishment of regiments. Like the Whites, they were accomplished looters, having lived off the countryside for so long that the peasants and townspeople had been reduced to starvation.

Once more the communist leaders could not make up their minds what sort of defence forces they wanted. The Red Army in 1922 contained the old and the new: Tsarist generals of the doctrinaire kind, senior commanders who were formerly young officers or non-commissioned officers, together with others, often barely literate, who had come from factory floor or field; old Bolsheviks and fanatical communists, former White officers, some foreign-trained, others the recent output from Red military schools. The equipment varied from the modern to the long obsolete, and was of Russian, Japanese, United States and British pattern. A few favoured a standing army, but most wanted a militia or loose guerrilla-type force under temporary or elected commanders.

Trotsky, possibly influenced by his military specialist advisers, wanted a return to an orthodox and regular army backed up by territorial reserve formations which in peacetime were to exist in a cadre form. But he was opposed by both the younger group of officer specialists such as Tukhachevsky and Uborevich, and, more important, by Frunze and other older revolutionaries with a military interest. The 'Tsaritsyn Group', led by Voroshilov and Budenny, were Trotsky's enemies, and when, after Lenin's death, Stalin used L. B. Kamenev and Zinoviev, his two colleagues in the governing triumvirate, to isolate Trotsky politically, the days of the Jewish Commissar for War were numbered. In 1924 Sklyansky, the Deputy Commissar for War and Trotsky's trusted aide, was replaced by Frunze. Antonov-Ovseenko, another of Trotsky's close collaborators, was replaced as chief commissar by Stalin's nominee Bubnov, formerly of 1 Cavalry Army. Stalin's henchman Voroshilov took over the command of the troops in the capital and together with Bubnov and Budenny was appointed to the Revolutionary Military Council.

Trotsky was now unprotected and in January 1925 was forced to hand over his post to Frunze. Tukhachevsky and Shaposhnikov, a former

A major of tanks or artillery talking to tank crews on 1937 manœuvres in the Belorussian Military District, probably part of a cavalry/mechanized division. (Novosti Press Agency)

colonel of the Imperial General Staff, were appointed as Frunze's deputies and S. S. Kamenev, until recently the Commander-in-Chief, became chief of the inspectorate. That year Frunze died unexpectedly. His death was certainly convenient to Stalin, for Voroshilov became the Commissar for War, a post he was to hold until 1940, and from 1928 onwards Shaposhnikov was chief of the newly redesignated General Staff.

Yet the opposition to Trotsky was based on personal and ideological grounds rather than on military logic; Trotsky's successors left the Red Army very much as they found it.

In the 1920s the Soviet defence forces were restricted to a ceiling of 562,000 men organized into thirty-one regular rifle divisions, ten regular cavalry divisions, and forty-six territorial reserve cadre divisions. There was neither the money nor the equipment for more. The officer in particular occupied a very depressed position; officer ranks, as such, were not in use, the very word 'officer' still being forbidden. Poorly paid, the officer messed with the rank and file and was expected to remove his commander's insignia when not on duty. The 1924–5 experiment of returning to the principle of one-man command in the event came to nothing, and real authority remained with the commissar.

Germany and the Soviet Union, both friendless in a very hostile world, were drawn together. Both distrusted a Poland reinforced by the Franco-Polish Entente. Thus, from 1921 there came about a fairly close collaboration between the Red and German Armies and between Moscow and the German armament industry. In exchange for training facilities in the Soviet Union, the Germans provided information, equipment and instructors, and the Red Army, like the Imperial Russian Army before it, began to take on a very heavy German bias in its organization, methods and terminology.

From 1927 onwards the Soviet Union professed to believe that it was once again threatened with foreign intervention and war. Its relationship with the West, particularly with Britain, was bad. The communist missions had been evicted from Nationalist China and the Chinese border clashes involving Blukher's Far East Forces were to become more numerous. Stalin intended at all costs to concentrate on the expansion of heavy industry and the re-equipment of his forces; and so the first of the Five Year Plans was born, aimed at establishing the Soviet Union among the foremost of the world's industrial powers. A large part of the new or redeployed industry was sited in the area of the Urals nearly 1,000 miles to the east of Moscow, outside the reach of the foreign interventionists. Soviet agriculture, at that time relatively inefficient, was later to be collectivized under state control in order to increase production, to redirect the surplus labour force into the factories and finally to break down the conservatism of a peasantry which was continually holding the nation to ransom by withholding its food supplies. This at least is how Stalin and the Soviet planners saw the problem. Their solution brought confiscations and deportations with mass starvation to the Ukraine and the North Caucasus. The Red Army was used to quell the riots which followed.

The early 1930s saw the gradual re-equipping and mechanization of the Red Army and its steady increase in size. Tukhachevsky had become Inspector of Armaments and Egorov had replaced Shapnoshnikov as Chief of General Staff. In Germany Hitler was in power and Europe was in a state of political turmoil. By 1934 all collaboration with Germany had been stopped. The Red Army now stood at nearly one million men and the Soviet Government began to take an even closer and more urgent interest in strengthening the morale and efficiency of its armed forces. That year the Commissariat of the Army and Navy was renamed the Commissariat of Defence and, in an effort to improve the morale and status of the military commanders, political commissars (except where they were members of the military councils of higher formations) were made subordinate to the military specialists. By 1935, in which year the Red Army had increased to 1,300,000 men, officers' ranks were reintroduced, except that the Red Army still had no generals, general officers being designated as 'brigade, division, corps or army commanders'. For the very word 'general', like that of 'officer', was still anathema to the old Bolsheviks. The officers' pay and conditions were greatly improved, and all but junior officers were granted immunity from civil arrest unless the arrest should be approved by the Commissar for Defence. This was the restoration of a dignity enjoyed by the officer in Tsarist times, but in the Soviet State it was meaningless, as subsequent purges were to show. Five Marshals of the Soviet Union were created during 1935: Voroshilov, Budenny, Tukhachevsky, Egorov and Blukher.

Meanwhile the mechanization and re-equipment of the armed forces were continued, and the leaders of the Red Army, uncertain of themselves and their military thinking, were urgently seeking contact with, and even reassurance from, military circles in Germany and France.

The Great Purges

Trotsky had been banished some years before, but Stalin still appeared intent upon ridding himself not only of those who at one time had been close to Trotsky and Lenin but of any who might be

A 1937 cavalry parade. (Novosti Press Agency)

in a position to challenge or undermine his own authority. To these were added those who in the past had done anything to incur his jealousy or displeasure. Yet the great purges, which probably destroyed millions of Soviet and foreign citizens, involved for the most part people in all walks of life of whose existence he was totally ignorant.

From the very earliest days Stalin's fortunes had rested in some degree on the influence he had over the Cheka secret police organization, renamed the OGPU in 1922, and then in 1934 the NKVD. So in 1936 Stalin, by now supreme dictator, instructed the NKVD to undertake its widespread investigation into the state of the Soviet Union; shortly afterwards he decided that much of the NKVD should be liquidated. Arrests followed investigations, with torture and execution or deportation, the NKVD being policeman, warder, judge and executioner, apparently accountable to no one but Stalin. Investigations led to confessions and denunciations, most of them false and intended only to protect the victim's family; and so the purge spread like wildfire and became the terror which Stalin probably intended it to be.

The first of the public trials opened in 1936, and Tukhachevsky was named, as if in an aside, in one of the confessions. Almost immediately Red Army leaders began to be arrested by the NKVD. Any senior leader who had criticized or crossed Stalin in earlier years was doomed, together with any who had been on friendly terms with the so-called opposition elements. Many commanders were arrested for no apparent reason. Tukhachevsky was executed and, of the eight members of the military tribunal who condemned him, six were to follow him to the death chamber. Only Budenny and Shaposhnikov survived. The other two of the five Marshals, Egorov and Blukher, were done away with. Thirteen army commanders and over 400 corps, divisional and brigade commanders were arrested and disappeared. Yet it is significant that the small Tsaritsyn Group and those associated with Budenny's 1 Cavalry Army in the Civil War were, with a few exceptions, retained in their posts.

Another reaction associated with the purge of the Red Army was the restoration of the political commissar to his pre-1934 position of equality with the military commander. Once more he could veto all orders.

World opinion of the power and effectiveness of the Red Army was not high. Not unnaturally, the prestige of the Soviet armed forces suffered further as a result of the purges. It was argued that the loss of so many of its high-ranking commanders must inevitably lead to a break in continuity and a grave loss in combat efficiency. Nor could the foreign policy or the political proposals of a dictator who appeared determined on slaughtering his own armed forces be taken seriously.

In 1937 Shaposhnikov returned to the post of Chief of General Staff and the following year the control of the Soviet Navy was separated from that of the Red Army and put under its own Defence Commissariat. The Red Air Force, however, remained as an integral part of the Red Army.

Soviet Expansionism and the Threat of War

In 1938 border fighting had broken out between the Japanese and troops of Blukher's Far East Front in the area of Lake Khasan near Vladivostok. In August of that year Blukher had been purged, in spite of the fact that his troops had been not unsuccessful. The Far East Front was broken up into two separate armies, one under Konev and the other under Shtern, who, shortly afterwards, was arrested in his turn. More fighting flared up, this time to the west of Manchuria in the area of Khalkhin-Gol. There Zhukov, a former Tsarist cavalry junior non-commissioned officer but by now an army commander, had been sent to the area to take command of operations. Fighting continued intermittently until September 1939.

The outbreak of war that month between Germany on the one side and Great Britain and France on the other brought to a head a number of outstanding military and political problems in the Soviet Union.

In September 1939 it was announced that henceforth the Red Army would be recruited from national servicemen who would be taken into the forces *irrespective of their social origin*. Previously, particularly in the late 'twenties and early 'thirties, recruits from a noble or middle-class background were discriminated against in that they were drafted into unarmed labour units where conditions of service were often particularly harsh. National service had been set at only two years, although non-commissioned officers had to serve for three, and the strength of the armed forces stood at just over two million men. That September, however, the conscription age was lowered from twenty-one to nineteen years so that a further two annual intakes each of about

A tank commander communicating by flags in 1937, a standard procedure even until late in the Second World War. The tank cannot be positively identified but was probably a T 28

1,400,000 men became eligible for service. Their call-up over the next two years had the effect of increasing Soviet armed strength, actually with the colours, to nearly five million men.

By the terms of the secret protocol signed by Molotov, the Soviet Commissar for Foreign Affairs, and von Ribbentrop, the German Foreign Minister, in Moscow on the night of 23 August 1939, the Balkans, Finland and the Baltic States were declared to be within the sphere of interest of the Soviet Union. Poland was to be partitioned between Germany and the USSR, the Soviet Union claiming those areas to the east where the population were of Ukrainian or White Russian stock. On 17 September 1939 the Red Army invaded Poland, the troops being deployed in two army groups or fronts, the Belorussian Front under Kovalev, and the Ukrainian Front under a Bessarabian Ukrainian, a former cavalry soldier of 1 Cavalry Army, by the name of Timoshenko. By then, however, the Polish forces had already been defeated by the Germans.

Immediately afterwards the Soviet Union, taking advantage of a situation in which British and French warships were excluded from the Baltic, demanded and was granted naval and military bases in Estonia, Latvia and Lithuania. A similar demand made on Finland and a proposal for an exchange of territory was rejected by Helsinki. This led to the Russo-Finnish Winter War.

The Russo-Finnish Winter War

The Soviet offensive against Finland was launched by Leningrad Military District under the command of Meretskov, a former factory worker and political commissar who had distinguished himself by his service with the large Soviet contingent in Republican Spain. His force, consisting of about twenty-five divisions with numerous tanks, had an overwhelming advantage in numbers and material over the Finnish troops deployed against it. The Red Air Force had an almost complete air superiority.

The Red Army offensive was made not only in the south from the area of Leningrad and Lake Ladoga but also from Ukhta across the central waist of Finland and in the far north near Petsamo. The Finnish troops, although few in number and with little artillery or armoured support, were better trained and far better led than the Red enemy. The short hours of daylight and the heavily forested areas restricted observation and robbed the Red Army of the benefit of its air, artillery and armoured support. The weather was unusually bitter and the Soviet columns, making little progress, suffered defeat and sometimes annihilation at the hands of almost insignificant numbers of Finns. The very poor showing of the Red Army troops did not go unnoticed in Berlin.

At the end of December the Soviet High Command was reorganized in an attempt to remedy what threatened to be a disastrous situation. Meretskov went to a lower appointment, to an army. A new North-West Front was set up to control operations and Timoshenko was given the overall command. More troops were moved up until the Red forces on the Finnish borders totalled over a million.

After a period of reorganization and retraining the new Soviet offensive reopened in early February with heavy and well co-ordinated artillery support. After a month of heavy battles the exhausted Finns, numbering as a nation no more than four million, were forced to sue for an armistice.

The early Red Army defeats in Finland were widely misinterpreted abroad. The rigours of terrain and climate were not properly understood, nor their effect on Ukrainian troops, many of whom were unfamiliar with forest or mountain. Red Army field leadership, imprisoned by its own narrow experience in the Civil War, was admittedly poor. But very few foreigners were aware of the excellence of the training and the very high fighting qualities and morale of the Finnish soldier. Operating in his own dark forests, mountains and swamps, he was much superior to the Russian and also, as subsequent events were to prove, to the German soldier.

Yet in Moscow the lessons were not lost. An investigation was carried out into the course and the failures of the war and a number of important reforms were introduced. Voroshilov lost to Timoshenko the appointment of Commissar for Defence, which he had held for fifteen years without great distinction. A newer, stricter disciplinary code was introduced. An attempt was made to improve the status, and presumably the morale, of the

Youthful Red Army men from the Bashkir Republic, once the territory of the Orenburg Cossacks. Although these soldiers are not Cossacks they are wearing Cossack-type caps and cloaks. They are armed with the PPSh automatic. (Imperial War Museum)

senior Red Army and Navy commanders by restoring the Tsarist ranks of general and admiral. There was a further amelioration in the pay and conditions of commanders in the higher ranks and the political commissar was demoted once more to a subordinate position *vis-à-vis* the military commander. Timoshenko, together with Shaposhnikov, still Chief of General Staff, and Kulik, an old revolutionary-cum-artillery officer and former member of the Tsaritsyn Group, a nonentity who was a favourite of Stalin, were all promoted to the rank of Marshal of the Soviet Union to fill the vacancies left by the dead Tukhachevsky, Egorov and Blukher.

The aftermath of the Russo-Finnish War was a reorganization of higher-ranking officers which brought them into the posts they were to hold at the outbreak of the war with Germany. Meretskov replaced Shaposhnikov, who was in declining health, as Chief of General Staff. Vatutin became the Deputy Chief of General Staff and Golikov the head of the GRU, the military intelligence directorate. Zhukov followed Timoshenko as the Commander of Kiev Military District. Two officers who had distinguished themselves in the Finnish War, Kirponos and Pavlov, were rapidly advanced, Kirponos to the command of Leningrad Military District, and Pavlov to the West Military District in Belorussia. And, since Meretskov proved unsatisfactory to Stalin as Chief of General Staff, he was replaced only a few months afterwards, in February 1941, by Zhukov who gave up his post in the Ukraine to Kirponos. Some of these officers were to achieve fame and fortune; others met their death either on the field of battle or in the NKVD death cellar.

A motor-cycle battalion, probably autumn 1941

The Trial of Strength— June 1941

Hitler, the German National Socialist dictator, had always intended to destroy the Soviet Union as a political state and immediately after the victory over France he had given orders for the preparation of war against the USSR. Just over three million German troops were allocated to the eastern front, a ground force of 140 divisions. Germany's allies, Finland, Romania and Hungary, furnished the equivalent of another forty divisions. The invasion force was supported by just over 2,000 first-line combat aircraft and included 3,500 tanks.

The preparations for the coming war could not be concealed from Moscow. Stalin, however, dismissed the reports as British and German provocation, or as part of the political war of nerves. Yet he did take some elementary precautions when he sanctioned a limited call-up of reservists in January and April of 1941. By that June, the Red Army stood at a total of 303 divisions of which about seventy were reserve divisions still in the process of mobilizing. About twenty divisions were deployed against the Finns and 150 divisions stood near the borders in west and south-west European Russia; the remainder of the forces were in the Far East, along the Turkish border or in the interior.

The real strength of the Red Army lay in the industrial capacity of the Soviet Union and the

1 Army Commander of Second Rank, c. 1926
2 Marshal of the Soviet Union, c. 1936
3 Lieutenant-General of Infantry, c. 1941

MICHAEL ROFFE

A

1 **Trooper of Cavalry, Summer Home Service Uniform, c. 1938**
2 **Private of Infantry, Winter Field Service Uniform, c. 1937**
3 **Private of Infantry, Summer Field Service Uniform, c. 1937**

B

MICHAEL ROFFE

1 **Major of Armoured Troops, Home Service Uniform, c. 1941**
2 **Private of Infantry, Ski Troops Winter Field Service Uniform, c. 1942**
3 **Colonel of the Red Air Force, Home Service Uniform, c. 1941**

MICHAEL ROFFE

C

1 **Sergeant of Armoured Troops, Parade Dress, c. 1945**
2 **Infantry Machine-Gunner, Winter Field Service Uniform, c. 1943**
3 **Army General in Parade Dress, c. 1944**

D

1 Warrant Officer of Infantry, Summer Field Service Order, c. 1953
2 Tank Commander Officer or Sergeant, Field Service Uniform, c. 1953
3 Lieutenant of Artillery, Summer Field Service Order, c. 1955

MICHAEL ROFFE

E

1 **Colonel of Infantry, Parade Dress, c. 1956**
2 **Private of Infantry, Winter Field Service Order, c. 1959**
3 **Private of Infantry, Tropical Field Service Uniform, c. 1960**

MICHAEL ROFFE

1 Captain of Engineers, Parade Uniform, c. 1960
2 Senior Sergeant (Extended Service) of Infantry, Parade Uniform, c. 1961
3 Lance-Corporal (Efreitor) of Infantry, Parade Uniform, c. 1961

1 Corporal (Junior Sergeant) of Infantry, Summer Battle Order, c. 1961
2 Private of Infantry in Summer Full Marching Order, 1961
3 Ceremonial Guard, c. 1967

MICHAEL ROFFE

great stockpile of armament prepared in the years immediately before the war. In 1941, according to what Stalin told Roosevelt's envoy, Harry Hopkins, the Red Army held 24,000 tanks and 7,000 combat planes, and the USSR had a production capacity of 12,000 tanks and 21,000 aircraft a year. Much of Soviet industry had already been moved eastward to the Urals and beyond. Both Hitler and German intelligence failed to appreciate not only the newly-found industrial and economic strength of the Soviet Union but also the extent of the scientific and technological advances already made in so backward a country.

It was true, of course, that the Red Army was to pay the price for over-production. The aircraft and most of the tanks were of obsolete or obsolescent pattern, for the Russian mentality, obsessed with numbers, consigned nothing to the scrap-heap. The Germans did this for them. But a new Soviet equipment series had already been accepted for service and was shortly to go into mass production and this included the KV and T 34 tanks, until 1943 the best in the world, and Yak 3 and Mig 3 fighters and the *Stormovik* Il 2 ground-attack fighter-bomber.

Despite the many indications of war, the invasion, when it came on 22 June 1941, took the Soviet High Command by surprise. Much of the Red Air Force was destroyed on the ground. Pavlov's West Front of fifty divisions covering Belorussia and the approaches to Moscow was virtually destroyed by encircling panzer columns in little more than a week. Pavlov and his staff were immediately arrested, transported to Moscow and shot by Stalin's orders. In the Ukraine, Kirponos was more successful in keeping his troops together and he resisted more strongly, but the Soviet losses were heavy as he fell back towards the Dnieper. In the area of the Baltic, German troops reached the Leningrad area after only a month or so of fighting.

All the signs seemed to show that the Soviet Union was about to undergo a fresh Stalin purge and terror. There was a wave of arrests of unsuccessful and unlucky Red Army commanders by the NKVD. Many of the field divisions had disintegrated at the first impact of battle, and NKVD detachments policed the roads to the rear, arresting officers and commissars and rounding up

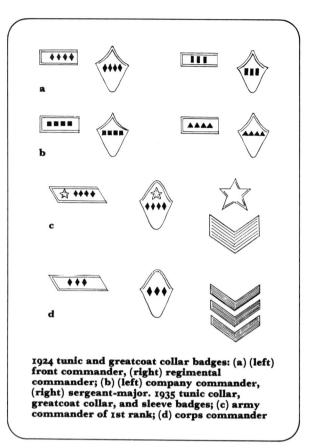

1924 tunic and greatcoat collar badges: (a) (left) front commander, (right) regimental commander; (b) (left) company commander, (right) sergeant-major. 1935 tunic collar, greatcoat collar, and sleeve badges; (c) army commander of 1st rank; (d) corps commander

the stragglers. Stalin himself assumed the posts of Chairman of the Defence Committee (the GKO) and Chairman of the Committee of the High Command, to which he gave the Tsarist designation of *Stavka*. Shortly afterwards the dictator assumed the function of Supreme Commander-in-Chief. Since he appeared to believe that the Red Army failures were due in part to the weakening of the authority of the political commissar he once more reversed the decisions taken after the Finnish War and restored the commissar to a position of parity with the military commander. So once again, as in Trotsky's day, all military orders were invalid unless signed by the political commissar.

Moscow 1941

Smolensk, on the direct road to Moscow and only 200 miles from the Kremlin, had fallen to the Germans on 17 July. Agitated and frightened,

Stalin's 'Tsaritsyn Group' all of whom were to reach high rank in the Red Army: Voroshilov, Budenny and Shchadenko. (Hulton)

Stalin sent the Red Army's most energetic and distinguished soldier, Marshal Timoshenko, to take over the field command in front of Moscow. Voroshilov was sent to Leningrad and Budenny to Kiev. But Hitler had meanwhile turned his main thrust away from the Moscow axis and down to the south in the Ukraine. There in early September Kirponos's South-West Front in the area of Kiev was almost destroyed with the loss of about 600,000 prisoners. Timoshenko, hurriedly dispatched from one trouble spot to another, was sent south, to replace Budenny in overall command in the Ukraine. Konev temporarily took over the West Front. Leningrad was in mortal danger and Zhukov was sent there to replace Voroshilov.

By the beginning of October the German forces had moved once more to the north and concentrated on the Moscow highway in the area of Smolensk. Hitler intended to advance rapidly eastward and occupy all territory west of a line from Archangel to Astrakhan, several hundred miles to the east of Moscow, before the onset of winter. The initial assault was highly successful,

destroying most of Konev's reconstituted West Front between Smolensk and Vyazma, and capturing 670,000 Red Army prisoners in the first fourteen days of the offensive.

Yet, although this was not realized either in Moscow or Berlin, the German Army had already shot its bolt and was shortly to be faced with failure and retreat. The infantry in particular had been thinned by casualties and had insufficient strength for its task in terms of extended frontages and distances. There was a scant margin of equipment reserves, and the supply system, based mainly on inefficiently operated and retracked railway lines supplemented by motor and horse transport, failed to keep pace with the ever-extending lines of communication. Before the start of the war the fighting value of the Red Army had been lightly regarded in Berlin, but the German troops had been surprised, not at the fighting efficiency of the Red soldier, which was still low, but at his stamina and obstinacy and at the ingenuity of his more senior leaders. But in the last resort what was to defeat the German 1941 autumn offensives was the onset of the heavy seasonal rains, the floods and the great seas of knee-deep, even waist-deep, mud which brought all tracked and wheeled movement to a halt. The mud broke up the very few roads there were, and stopped everything except air supply, while the *Luftwaffe* air transport force was quite inadequate in size to maintain even a small part of the German ground forces.

As conditions worsened for the bogged-down German troops, the Red Army appeared to take heart and daily to become stronger and bolder. After the Vyazma disaster, Zhukov had been recalled from Leningrad to take over the West Front and there began a period of frantic reorganization and movement of reinforcement formations from the Far East Maritime Provinces to meet the renewal of the German offensive which, as the Kremlin knew, must come as soon as the November frosts had hardened the ground again.

Hitler's final 1941 offensive was near-disastrous to the German troops. In bitter cold, without winter clothing or equipment or any reserves of troops or ammunition, the three German army groups in the east attacked eastward towards Tikhvin and Finland, Moscow and the Caucasus. The Red Army defenders, unlike the Tsarist forces or their fathers in the White or Red Guards during the Civil War, were tolerably well clothed and armed despite the previous summer's enormous losses in equipment. By the first week in December the German troops had come to a final halt in Tikhvin, in the Moscow outskirts hardly

Red Air Force officer crews in front of an ER 2 medium bomber, probably in 1942. (Imperial War Museum)

twenty miles from the Kremlin, and in Rostov, the gateway to the Caucasus. A week later they were pulling back with the Red Army in pursuit. Army Group Centre, to the west of Moscow, in constant danger of encirclement and destruction, retreated over the next three months nearly 200 miles to the west. Not before the beginning of April was the German line stabilized.

The Red Army had successfully withstood one year of war and, at great cost to itself, had inflicted a serious check on the *Wehrmacht*. German losses in the east in this first year of war totalled nearly 300,000 dead and missing and 800,000 wounded. In addition the bitter winter weather and the effects of exposure without proper clothing had caused the admission of nearly half a million sick to hospital; of these, the 228,000 frostbite cases were likely to result in prolonged, or permanent, absence from duty. The Red Army losses for the first year of war have never been admitted but were probably in the region of six million; the Germans held over three million Red Army men prisoners.

Stalingrad

By 1942 Hitler had lost interest in taking Moscow or advancing to the Archangel–Astrakhan line. Instead he decided to occupy the industrial area of the Donets Basin in the East Ukraine and secure for Germany the rich deposits of oil in the Caucasus. To this master strategic plan the Führer

A commissar (note the star and hammer-and-sickle device on the left sleeve) of the Red Air Force reading Stalin's order of the day from *Pravda*. Date probably 1 May 1942

A senior lieutenant of cavalry in the home service tunic, wearing his braces crossed. His horse is snaffle- and not Pelham-bitted. Date 1942. (Imperial War Museum)

began to add subsidiary tasks, an advance to the Turkish frontier, the capture of the Black Sea naval ports and the cutting of the Volga river and rail traffic in the area of Tsaritsyn, renamed Stalingrad since 1925.

Meanwhile Stalin and Timoshenko had been preparing their own major summer offensive; by chance they had chosen exactly the same sector on which the initial German attack was to fall. The Red Army completed its preparations first; in May 1942 the South and South-West Fronts struck a massive blow in the area to the south-east of Kharkov. The Red Army had a considerable initial success. But the German counter-offensive caught them unawares, and within a week the South-West Front had been decisively defeated with a loss of 200,000 prisoners. Subsequent operations developed into a rapid pursuit which took the Germans 400 miles to the east, to the Volga and Stalingrad and to the summit of the Caucasus.

Yet, by the autumn of 1942, the city of Stalingrad had still not been completely cleared, for the Red Army enemy hung on tenaciously to part of the western bank. The Volga river traffic had admittedly been stopped up, but little oil had been captured in the Caucasus, as the oil fields had been handed over to the fire-raisers. Yet from the Soviet side the situation appeared very grave.

After the summer defeats Timoshenko had lost his command. He was to continue to hold active appointments but his star was already on the wane. Budenny and Voroshilov had been discredited as field commanders and had now been relegated to training or organizing inspectorates. Shaposhnikov had finally, in midsummer 1942, resigned his post of Chief of General Staff to Vasilevsky, a comparatively unknown general staff officer. Zhukov, still with the West Front, had been appointed Deputy Supreme Commander and detached to the Stalingrad area. The front commanders in the Volga–Don area were all new men, most of them from the cavalry, Vatutin, Rokossovsky, Malinovsky and Eremenko. With them was Stalin's henchman, commissar Khrushchev, forging a new and second Tsaritsyn Group, a clique bound by personal associations and loyalties to Khrushchev, to whom some of them were to owe their high appointments after Stalin's death.

At Hitler's order the German troops of 6 Army, impervious to mounting casualties, continued their fanatical attacks on the burnt-out shell of Stalingrad. Commanded, even bullied, by Stalin, Eremenko's Red Army men held doggedly on to the narrow rubble-strewn strip of the Volga right bank. But the German defeat came not in the ruins of Stalingrad but far to the rear on the right Don flank, which was held by Romanian, Italian and Hungarian troops. For while Eremenko held the Germans on the Volga, Vatutin and Rokossovsky mounted a November joint offensive southward across the Don, aimed at linking up with Eremenko's left flank. The German allies could not hold and only four days after the attack Paulus's 6 German Army and part of 4 Panzer Army had been encircled at Stalingrad.

Paulus might have broken out, but the German dictator ordered that he remain. No German

Parachutists about to take off. Note the second chest parachute. (Novosti Press Agency)

reserves were available to mount an immediate relief operation and by the time that they had been assembled they themselves were in danger of encirclement by further Soviet offensives mounted higher up the Don. By 2 February 1943 the whole of the Stalingrad enclave had been overrun by Rokossovsky's troops, and 6 Army, made up of over twenty German divisions, had been destroyed. Between 200,000 and 300,000 German troops were permanently lost.

This was the first great victory of the war won by the Red Army and its most significant aspect was the ability with which the Soviet High Command and the more senior field commanders handled the large tank and mechanized forces. Much cavalry remained, however, for large numbers of Red cavalry divisions forming part of the mobile troops took part in the offensive and were to continue in being until the end of the war. In the German Army, on the other hand, the only cavalry division in the entire order of battle had already been converted to a panzer division.

Now came a full return to the Imperial Army of the Tsars. The rank designation of 'officer' was introduced. New officer uniforms appeared with braid and shoulder-board epaulettes, the new rank insignia being so close to that of the 1914 Russian Army that if any of the former generals murdered by the Bolsheviks could have been restored to life and rank, they would have felt thoroughly at home. The wheel had turned full circle.

There was a general relaxation of political tension and the military commanders of formations and units, lower than those of the army, became solely responsible for their own actions; the political commissars were once more subordinate to the military.

From Victory to Victory

After Stalingrad the Red Army never lost a major battle; the *Wehrmacht* never won a lasting success. The German troops fell back rapidly from the Caucasus into the Ukraine. Hitler's obdurate insistence on rigidly holding ground gave the Red enemy the tactical and strategic initiative. The

A colonel wearing the 1943 shoulder-boards and the Order of the Red Banner. Since this is in black and white his arm cannot be identified. (Imperial War Museum)

dispersal of German troops over Western Europe, Scandinavia, the Mediterranean and the whole of the thousand-mile-long eastern front rendered both troops and resources insufficient for the task in hand. Meanwhile Soviet armament production continued to rise, the 1944 figures totalling 29,000 tanks and 32,000 aircraft of all types.

In July 1943 the German Führer mounted his last major offensive in the east at the battle of Kursk, aimed at enveloping Rokossovsky's and Vatutin's fronts. The offensive was a bloody and costly failure; the Germans made no further attempt to regain the strategic initiative.

Throughout the remainder of 1943 and until the middle of 1944 fierce fighting continued about Leningrad and the Belorussian borderlands. But the main German defeats were in the forced evacuation of the Ukraine; the battles at Cherkasy-Korsun and the Crimea caused heavy German losses. By June 1944 the Russians were on the

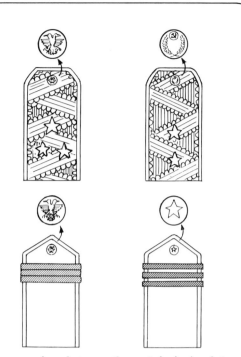

A comparison between the rank insignia of the Imperial Russian Army in 1914 and the Red Army in 1943. (Top: left) Lieutenant-general of the Imperial Army, three silver stars on crimson piping with double-headed eagle on brass button, background all of gold lace; (right) lieutenant-general of the Red Army, two silver stars with piping and background of the 1914 colour but with five bars of piping instead of six; and the brass button carries a laurel wreath device. (Below: left) The 1914 sergeant of guard infantry has the double eagle button, three orange bars on an olive-khaki background, and a border of green piping; (right) the 1943 button is a five-pointed star, the separate bars are claret against a khaki background, and the piping is magenta

another strategic command controlling the two fronts which invaded Romania in August 1944. The Romanians had in fact already sought peace. The reconstituted 6 German Army inside Romania was enveloped and encircled, and about 180,000 men disappeared. Within a matter of weeks Red Army troops had crossed the Romanian borders into Hungary and part of Yugoslavia.

By the beginning of 1945 Anglo-American forces were on the Rhine while the Red Army lined the Vistula in Poland. German troops had been driven out of the Baltic States and were defending East Prussia.

The last two major operations of the war on the eastern front involved the fighting across Poland from the Vistula to the Oder and then, after a pause for build-up and reorganization, the final offensive from the Oder, across Mecklenburg, Brandenburg and Saxony, to the Elbe, where a junction was made with Anglo-American troops. For this final phase of the war Vasilevsky, having given up his post as Chief of General Staff to Antonov, took the overall command of operations to reduce East Prussia, where German troops held out with bitter fanaticism. Zhukov was in command of the front to the west of Berlin. Zhukov's 1 Belorussian and Konev's 1 Ukrainian Fronts included ten armies, of which two were tank, and which jointly numbered 163 divisions, 6,400 tanks, 4,700 aircraft and 2,200,000 men. About the same number of men were involved in the Oder operation.

So ended what was probably the greatest war in the long history of Germany and Russia. German losses on the eastern front from June 1941 to April 1945 numbered 1,001,000 dead, 3,966,000 wounded and 1,288,000 missing, in all just over six million. The Red Army casualties have never been given but, including the known six million prisoners, probably amounted in all to about fourteen million men.

The Far East

Because the Soviet Union had political and territorial pretensions in the Far East, Stalin was anxious to be in at the kill when the Japanese

Romanian border. That month, shortly after the Anglo-Americans had landed in Normandy, Zhukov and Vasilevsky, co-ordinating operations in Belorussia, East Poland and Galicia, and by then both Marshals of the Soviet Union, gained one of the greatest victories of the war when they enveloped and almost completely destroyed Busch's Army Group Centre, twenty-eight divisions strong, where the German losses totalled nearly 300,000 men. In the far north near Leningrad another newly promoted Marshal, Govorov, once a White Guard officer, attacked both into the Baltic and into Finland, forcing the Finns out of the war.

In the south, Timoshenko had been given

A 45 mm anti-tank in action, probably in 1943. Note the quilted clothing of the crew. (Imperial War Museum)

Empire was destroyed. Yet in fact the United States no longer needed Soviet help in overcoming Japan and regarded Soviet participation with some mistrust.

As soon as the war against Germany had been ended, Red Army formations were moved to the Far East until the build-up there totalled about eighty divisions of 1,600,000 men with a very large tank component. Vasilevsky was appointed to the overall command, the three new fronts (the Trans-baikal and 1 and 2 Far East Fronts) being commanded by Malinovsky, Meretskov and Purkaev, another veteran of the fighting against the Germans.

By then, however, the Japanese had already put out feelers for peace. On 6 and 9 August 1945 the two atomic bombs were dropped from United States aircraft on Hiroshima and Nagasaki; the Red Army troops, bringing forward their invasion date, crossed the Manchurian frontier. The campaign, such as it was, lasted only five days during which there was much movement but only limited fighting, and on 14 August the Japanese surrendered unconditionally to all the allies.

The Soviet Army

In March 1946 Stalin, who had delved into Tsarist history to provide for himself the military rank of *Generalissimo*, handed over his post as Commissar for Defence to Bulganin, a trusted party member and henchman who had served throughout the war as a political commissar with the Red Army and was said, at the time of the Civil War, to have been a Chekist. The name, 'The Red Army', was abolished at about this time and replaced by the new title of 'The Soviet Army'.

The High Command remained little altered. Vasilevsky returned to his old post as Chief of General Staff, henceforth known as the General Staff of the Soviet Army and Navy, and Antonov slipped down to become once more his deputy. A new post had been created, the Chief of the Soviet Ground Forces, held first by Zhukov until by Stalin's order he was relegated to obscurity, and then by Konev. Marshal Sokolovsky, a former front commander and chief of staff, commanded the Soviet troops in Germany while Rokossovsky was Commander-in-Chief in Poland. Three years later, however, in 1949, Stalin reorganized the High Command once more. The Soviet Navy, which had been controlled from the Ministry of Defence since 1941, was hived off yet again and separate Ministries of War and of the Navy came into being, replacing the Ministry of Defence. Bulganin lost his appointment and Vasilevsky returned to Moscow to become Chief of General Staff.

At the beginning of 1953, with the so-called discovery of the doctors' plot, there was reason to believe that another great purge was pending in the Soviet Union. Even Molotov, Mikoyan and Voroshilov were said to be in danger of their lives. Within the month Stalin was dead.

A Modern Army

In the interval between the First and the Second World Wars Stalin and his principal military leaders, Voroshilov, Budenny and Tukhachevsky, had been obsessed with their military experiences and what they chose to call the lessons of the Civil War. For none of them had seen any real fighting against the Central Powers. After 1945 Stalin and his military staffs lived and relived the battles of the Second World War, and for many years appeared to disregard the possible effect of atomic or nuclear weapons on the development of armed forces. Meanwhile every effort was made completely to mechanize the armed forces, for the greater part of the Red Army in 1945 had still relied on horse-drawn transport and guns. The mass production of new tanks, armoured carriers and radio was also given great priority, so that by the mid-'fifties the Soviet Army began to take on the new image of a heavily armoured and motorized force. In the event, almost by accident rather than far-sighted design, the Soviet Union had developed ground forces suitable for both nuclear and non-nuclear war.

In 1953 the USSR fired a nuclear device and, four years later, its first intercontinental ballistic missile. Shortly after 1957 the first tactical and field strategic missiles began to appear with the ground forces.

Following Stalin's death the Ministry of Defence, again under Bulganin, replaced the Ministries of War and of the Navy, with Vasilevsky as the First Deputy and Zhukov as the Second Deputy and Commander of the Ground Forces. Govorov, an artillery officer, remained as Commander of the Air Defences. Two years later the collective leadership began to break up, Khrushchev emerging as the dominant figure with Bulganin as the titular Premier. Zhukov became

Red Army cavalry near Kursk late 1943. (Imperial War Museum)

Minister for Defence. Khrushchev's second Tsaritsyn Group then came to the fore. Marshal Malinovsky became the Commander of the Ground Forces and Eremenko, Bagramyan, Chuikov, Grechko and others who had been closely associated with Khrushchev on the Volga and the Don and in the Ukraine were rapidly promoted to Marshal's rank. Before the end of 1956, however, Khrushchev had begun to find the arrogant and loud-mouthed Zhukov both an inconvenience and an embarrassment, particularly as he may have relied on Zhukov's support during his struggle for power. Zhukov was removed from all his offices, being replaced as Minister of Defence by Malinovsky. Grechko became the Chief of the Ground Forces.

By 1957 the Soviet Army had become completely modernized, backed by a strong fighter, bomber, ground-attack, air transport and helicopter force. It was still a conscript army, the recruit being called up at the age of nineteen and serving for three years before being discharged to the reserve. Marriage allowance was not normally

Artillery teams bringing up limbers loaded with ammunition and saddlery, c. 1943. (Imperial War Museum)

admissible and a private soldier's pay was about 30 roubles or £3 a month (compared with a major's pay of £200 and a major-general's of over £400 a month). A soldier's life was no more popular in the Soviet Army than it was in the Tsarist Army and it proved difficult, and sometimes impossible, to induce trained soldiers to extend their service, in spite of the very attractive monetary awards and a greatly inflated rate of pay for extended servicemen. The pattern of military

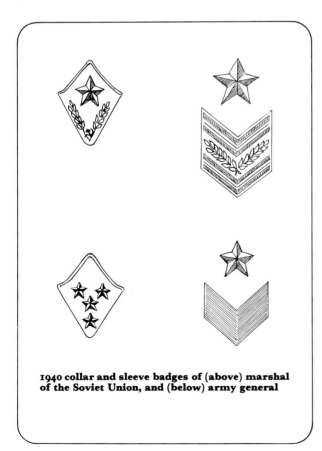

1940 collar and sleeve badges of (above) marshal of the Soviet Union, and (below) army general

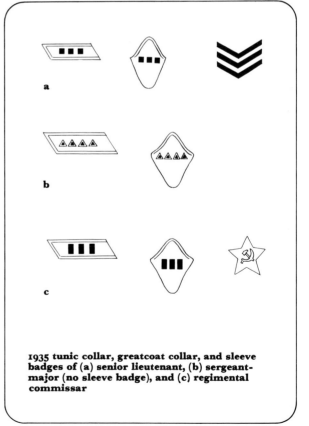

1935 tunic collar, greatcoat collar, and sleeve badges of (a) senior lieutenant, (b) sergeant-major (no sleeve badge), and (c) regimental commissar

A Josef Stalin 2 tank in 1945, the most powerful Red Army tank of the war. (Imperial War Museum)

conscription in 1957 was in fact little different from that in Tsarist days before the First World War. There was virtually no reserve of officers, except the elderly who had been retired on account of age, and there was no corps of long-service non-commissioned officers.

In some respects the Russian soldier had changed little since Tsarist days. He was cheerful and hardy, yet at the same time, unless kept to his duty, lethargic and apathetic. Propaganda and the presence of secret informers had made him, if anything, even more suspicious than his grandfather. He lived in fear of the communist régime, yet was sufficiently credulous to believe what it told him. He was still prone to rapid changes of mood. In many respects still very primitive, he had a flair for improvisation; he was different from the earlier generation in that he often had considerable mechanical aptitude and could usually read and write Russian. Many of the recruits had an advanced education.

The military command system, introduced by Trotsky as a temporary measure and bitterly attacked by Stalin at the time, had apparently stood the test of the years, for it remained in 1957 very much as Trotsky and Lenin had designed it. In addition the Soviet Army, in common with all the armed forces, contained as part of its permanent organization organs of the secret police, known before the war as the NKVD and subsequently as the KGB. The commissar was a professional commissioned military officer with additional and specialized political training; he wore the military uniform and rank badges of the arm to which he was accredited, and his true identity was seen only by the stitched red star and hammer-and-sickle emblem on his sleeve. The NKVD/KGB policeman, on the other hand, wore the uniform and insignia of any arm he pleased.

The year 1957 left the Soviet Army and the other armed forces in a state of continued reorganization. For the Soviet Union was in the throes of forming a fifth arm, the Strategic Rocket Forces, separate from the air, air defence, ground, and naval forces. The actual peacetime size of the Soviet Army at this time has been generally

Red Army infantry near Königsberg 1945, supported by a SU 76 AFV (a 76 mm gun on a T 70 chassis). (Imperial War Museum)

assumed by western commentators to be about 175 divisions, with a war reserve potential of perhaps double this figure. The same commentators now believe that the introduction of the Strategic Rocket Forces together with the difficulty in manning the increasingly complex modern equipment may have resulted in a substantial reduction in the peace strength of the ground forces below this figure.

Uniforms

Until about 1940, the uniforms of the Red Army were among the simplest in the world and, except for the very few orders and medals awarded by the Soviet government, bore no decoration or colour except for that of the red star, the badges of rank and the colour patches of the arm of service. In the attempt to emphasize the break with the old Tsarist régime, the wearing of swords, shoulder-boards and gold and silver braid was condemned

as relics of reactionary imperialism. The old pattern swords soon reappeared, however, and by 1924 few of the old revolutionaries on the saluting base in Red Square did not feel out of place without one.

The new rank designations and badges were admittedly much different from those of pre-war days. Yet the new revolutionary army soon began to take on many of the aspects and customs of the old. Most of the equipment dated before 1914. The infantryman carried the greatcoat slung over the left shoulder or strapped round the pack; bayonet scabbards were dispensed with and the bayonet was always carried fixed to the rifle. The cavalryman always slung the carbine over the left shoulder; Cossacks, when re-formed in 1936, continued, as in Tsarist days, to wear the rifle over the right. The Cossacks took the colours of their old Hosts, scarlet for the Don, crimson for the Kuban, and light blue for the Terek. Officers' ranks were eventually reintroduced. From October 1935 onwards there was a movement away from the previous policy of providing the soldier with a

A Red Army Command group in Budapest 1956 sandwiched between two APCs BR 152. A colonel of artillery advances threateningly on the photographer, drawing his pistol as he does so. Behind him a colonel of tank troops is shouting. The officer on the far left is a tank man. The others appear to be infantrymen. (Hulton)

uniform with the minimum of regard for ornamental effect; now a close fitting jacket and slacks were approved for officers and extended servicemen for both walking-out and evening wear. By 1941 this second uniform was being produced in different colours and varying designs for different arms, blue for the air force and dark grey for the armoured and mechanized troops. Rank badges were altered once more.

At the beginning of 1943 a new pattern of uniform was introduced, based on that used in Tsarist times. The word 'officer' was taken back into use; the broad shoulder-boards in gold and silver were worn once more, those for general

officers and non-commissioned officers being so close to those of a generation before that the uninformed observer could hardly tell the difference. Uniforms, for officers and extended servicemen, became more colourful.

This trend continued after the Second World War. In 1955 and 1959 there were further changes which introduced a new range of uniforms and modernized the design of the older patterns. As the new were added to the old, the Soviet Army began to appear in a wide variety of dress which has made identification and categorization a very intricate task. This process has continued into the 'sixties and the 'seventies.

The Plates

A1 Army Commander of Second Rank, c. 1926

This commander, who in 1926 was not entitled to call himself either general or officer, had in fact the rank equivalent to that of the latter-day colonel-general. He wears the plain Red Army cloth shako with side flaps which can be let down to cover the ears and the back of the neck, and his greatcoat is of a rough, soldier pattern almost like a heavy blanket in texture. This has no buttons but is secured with lines of hooks so that additional underclothing can be worn in winter. The four rhomboids on the collar patch are the only insignia of rank. The Order of the Red Banner is worn on the left breast without a ribbon. The sword is of particular interest since it is of Tsarist pattern, the red stitching on the scabbard possibly indicating that it is of Cossack origin from the old Caucasian Line Host. More interesting still is the fact that the scabbard is being worn back to front. A photograph taken two years before in Red Square showed that hardly any two senior officers dressed alike, some apparently having their belts on upside down.

A2 Marshal of the Soviet Union, c. 1936

This was the first of the general officer ranks to be taken into use. The star has appeared as an insignia of rank, together with gold braid and sleeve chevrons. Decorations are no longer worn on the greatcoat, but the main difference from plate A1 is in the quality of the senior officer's clothing.

A3 Lieutenant-General of Infantry, c. 1941

By 1941 the collar rank badges for all general officers carried stars instead of rhomboids, the background colour of the collar patch for ranks of colonel-general and below differing according to arm, crimson for infantry, blue for cavalry, light blue for air force and black for artillery and armour. The uniform, well cut and of good quality cloth, was the forerunner of that to appear in 1943 as a general issue for all officers. Rank can be distinguished both by the collar patch and the sleeve chevron. This officer's decorations, read from the top and from left to right, show him to be a deputy to the Supreme Soviet of the USSR, and to have been awarded the Order of Lenin, the Order of the Red Banner and the Red Star, and the Medal for Twenty Years' Service in the Red Army.

B1 Trooper of Cavalry, Summer Home Service Uniform, c. 1938

In 1938 the Soviet Union had the largest cavalry force in the world. and, together with the artillery, it was probably the best disciplined and trained arm of the Red Army. The cavalryman no longer carried the Tsarist lance but was armed with the M 20 7·62 mm Mosin Nagan carbine, which was a shorter version of the 91/30 rifle, and, like the Tsarist cavalry, carried a bayonet as well as the Tsarist (or the later universal pattern 27) sabre. When fighting dismounted, he usually left the sword on the saddle. Some soldiers, whose duties required it, were armed with the Nagan revolver rather than the carbine. The French-pattern steel helmet was very common at about this time. Horse furniture consisted of leather Tsarist dragoon saddles, numnahs and webbing girths, sometimes leather surcingles, and the double bridle Pelham port-mouth bits similar to those used by British cavalry. Rifles were always slung over the left shoulder to distinguish cavalry from Cossacks.

B2 Private of Infantry, Winter Field Service Uniform, c. 1937

This typical conscript on the march is equipped with the 91/30 Mosin Nagan rifle (see also plate B1). His right and left ammunition pouches do not match and he has removed his water-bottle from the hooks at the back of his belt, thrusting the cover flap through his waistband. A respirator is slung over his right shoulder. One of the features of the Red Army at this time (as of the old Imperial Army) was lack of uniformity of pattern of equipment and dress, even within the same unit. Several patterns of steel helmet existed, but the type shown here later became the standard type.

B3 Private of Infantry, Summer Field Service Uniform, c. 1937

Except for his forage-cap (*pilotka*), this infantry private is hardly to be distinguished from a soldier in Tsarist times. The pullover tunic (*gimnasterka*) was used before the First World War and the belt and equipment are of Tsarist pattern, together with the method of carrying the rolled greatcoat either strapped to the pack or thrown across the left shoulder. The ammunition pouches are, however, of Soviet pattern although these also are very similar to those used in 1914. The rifle is of the ·299 inch 1891 pattern (mounted type) with a bolt action and five-round magazine, which in 1930 was mass-produced as the Mosin Nagan M 91/30 taking the 7·62 mm round. It is four feet long, five feet five inches long with the bayonet fixed, and is effective up to about 600 yards. The bayonet was normally carried fixed and not in a scabbard. The steel helmet was not a general issue even in war-time.

C1 Major of Armoured Troops, Home Service Uniform, c. 1941

Whereas crimson (later magenta) has always distinguished infantry from other arms, the air force have worn light blue; the cavalry, blue; artillery and engineers, black; and armoured troops, black velvet; this latter colour being associated with grey. Rank can be read off from the collar patches and cuff chevrons.

C2 Private of Infantry, Ski Troops Winter Field Service Uniform, c. 1942

Ski troops were used to good effect against the German winter retreat before Moscow, for harassing and long-range penetration, carrying little equipment and relying on the local population to provide food and shelter. An entrenching tool, however, is carried by this soldier, together with a haversack and a M 40 Tokarev gas-operated self-loading rifle.

C3 Colonel of the Red Air Force, Home Service Uniform, c. 1941

The Red Air Force is a component of the Red Army and did not exist as a separate independent arm. In the field it wore khaki uniform with the light-blue facings on the arm of service patches.

This particular home service uniform, except in the colour of the material, is the same as that worn by the armoured troops (plate C1). The only decoration, the Order of the Red Star, worn by this colonel in 1941 on the left breast, was later to be worn on the right breast.

D1 Sergeant of Armoured Troops, Parade Dress, c. 1945

This sergeant is carrying the 7·62 mm M 40 Degtyarev LMG used both by infantry and armoured fighting vehicles. It is a gas-operated air-cooled weapon with a folding bipod and an effective range of perhaps 800 yards. It is fitted with a 50-round drum magazine. The soldier's medals include, on the right breast, a Second Class Order of the Fatherland War, and on his left, the Order of Glory Class Three, the Medal for Victory over Germany and the Berlin Medal.

D2 Infantry Machine-Gunner, Winter Field Service Uniform, c. 1943

During the Second World War the field service uniform consisted of a wide variety of clothing, depending on what was available. In the coldest of weather the more fortunate had quilted clothing and felt boots. But some, like this machine-gunner photographed at the time of Stalingrad, were provided only with essentials: a 7·62 mm PPSh M 1941 sub-machine-gun without bayonet with the 70-round drum magazine; a fur cap of lamb's-wool with let-down ear flaps; a greatcoat; ankle boots and puttees, possibly of English origin; a tie-up knapsack which serves as pack and a mess and cooking tin. His machine-gun, which he and his number two will drag into action, is an old pattern Maxim M 10 7·62 mm water-cooled and recoil-operated, fired from the wheeled carriage and trail. It has an effective range of about 2,000 yards.

D3 Army General in Parade Dress, c. 1944

This particular pattern dress in olive-khaki was later to appear in dark blue. It is designed very much on Tsarist lines with the old Imperial shoulder-boards in gold lace. The wearer, who like many of his rank is in his early forties, is wearing the scarlet ribbon and insignia of the Gold Star, this indicating that he is a Hero of the Soviet Union and a holder of the Order of Lenin; his medal ribbons show that he also holds the Order of Suvorov Second Class, the Order of Bogdan Khmelnitsky First Class and the Order of the Red Star.

E1 Warrant Officer of Infantry, Summer Field Service Order c. 1953
When full marching order was not carried the greatcoat was slung across the left shoulder. The soldier who, as indicated by his long-service medal, now worn on the right breast, has already served twenty years in the Red Army, is armed with the M 44 7·62 mm carbine with a permanently attached folding bayonet.

E2 Tank Commander Officer or Sergeant, Field Service Uniform, c. 1953
Since 1941 tank crews could be recognized easily by their dark clothing and distinctive tank helmet which is padded and fur-lined, with protective ribs for the top of the head. In the 'fifties radio earpieces and a throat-speaker were being incorporated into the design. Tank crews wore a dark-brown or black leather jacket, sometimes with loose overall trousers, or alternatively a set of black button-up overalls similar, except for the colour, to those worn by Soviet parachute troops.

E3 Lieutenant of Artillery, Summer Field Service Order, c. 1955
This officer is in an observation post waiting to accompany attacking infantry on to their objective. He controls the supporting fire of his own battery and other artillery that might be linked in with the radio net, through the man-pack radio station which he carries on his back. He usually has a single earpiece and a microphone receiver on a face frame. His pistol might be a 7·6 mm M 33, looking very much like a United States Service Colt, or possibly a 9 mm Makarov blowback automatic. The officer is wearing the khaki-backed field service shoulder-boards.

F1 Colonel of Infantry, Parade Dress, c. 1956
By 1956 there was a proliferation of new uniforms. This steel-grey uniform is for field and junior officers, whereas generals wore a very similar uniform in dark blue. The dress as worn here is for evening wear or for informal occasions. For parades, orders and medals are worn along the left lapel, instead of the medal ribbons, together with a gold and white silk belt to which is attached an ornamental dagger or dirk.

F2 Private of Infantry, Winter Field Service Order, c. 1959
A new pattern of pack, brace and harness has come into use and the greatcoats are now dark grey instead of khaki. The rifle is the self-loading 7·62 mm Simonov with a folding bayonet permanently attached to the rifle.

F3 Private of Infantry, Tropical Field Service Uniform, c. 1960
This soldier is equipped with the Simonov rifle (bayonet folded) and is in light tropical order wearing the desert camouflage suit with hood. The suit can be tucked into the boots. The distinctive cap is worn in summer by troops in Central Asia.

G1 Captain of Engineers, Parade Uniform, c. 1960
Black has for long been the basic arms colour for technical troops. The field engineers and sappers, whose arm of service badge was a crossed-axes device, appear to have been absorbed into a general engineer corps which includes bridging, construction, works and electrical units. The new arm of service badge is an amalgam of a circular-saw blade, bulldozers, axes, anchors and electrical lightning.

G2 Senior Sergeant (Extended Service) of Infantry, Parade Uniform, c. 1961
The Red Army and the Soviet Army, like the Imperial Tsarist Army before them, have had no corps of regular warrant and non-commissioned officers and have relied on extended-service conscripts to fill these appointments. As in Tsarist times there is difficulty in persuading conscripts to extend their service in spite of financial and other encouragements. The 1959 Dress Regulations provided the extended-service soldier with another inducement in the form of a parade dress very much like that of an officer. The issue of this uniform was later to be extended to other categories.

G3 Lance-corporal (Efreitor) of Infantry, Parade Uniform, c. 1961

This *Efreitor*, or private first class, is wearing the issue uniform for conscripts. Sometimes additional coloured gorget patches are worn on the collar of the tunic. His fully automatic machine-carbine (sub-machine-gun) is the Kalashnikov, originally a copy of the German 7·92 mm machine pistol 43 which it much resembles in design. The Soviet weapon fires 7·62 mm standard rimless ammunition and has good range and stopping power. It has been produced in several varieties of pattern. It can be fitted with a bayonet.

H1 Corporal (Junior Sergeant) of Infantry, Summer Battle Order, c. 1961

The traditional Tsarist *gimnastërka* is still in use together with khaki field shoulder-boards of a type which first appeared in 1914 and were used again during the Second World War. The rank badges are in red and not gold or claret. The equipment, which is partly of leather and partly of plastic-covered webbing, is of a new pattern. The soldier is armed with the Kalashnikov fully automatic machine-carbine.

H2 Private of Infantry in Summer Full Marching Order, 1961

The mainstay of the infantry section is the Simonov-rifle-armed private, loaded with respirator, water-bottle, entrenching tool, pack and folded greatcoat, ammunition pouches and grenade holders.

H3 Ceremonial Guard, c. 1967

This soldier on ceremonial guard duty in the capital is wearing a uniform which would not normally be found in ordinary units. The fur cap with its let-down ear-flaps is of excellent quality. The stylish and well-cut greatcoat is shown by the 1959 Regulations to be one of officers' pattern as is the gilt belt. The silk scarf is another unusual addition.

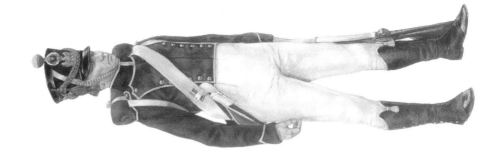

OSPREY
PUBLISHING

FIND OUT MORE ABOUT OSPREY

❑ Please send me a FREE trial issue
  of Osprey Military Journal

❑ Please send me the latest listing of Osprey's publications

❑ I would like to subscribe to Osprey's e-mail newsletter

Title/rank

Name

Address

Postcode/zip   state/country

e-mail

Which book did this card come from?

❑ I am interested in military history

My preferred period of military history is _____

❑ I am interested in military aviation

My preferred period of military aviation is _____

I am interested in *(please tick all that apply)*

❑ general history   ❑ militaria   ❑ model making
❑ wargaming   ❑ re-enactment

Please send to:

USA & Canada: Osprey Direct USA, c/o Motorbooks
International, P.O. Box 1, 729 Prospect Avenue, Osceola,
WI 54020

UK, Europe and rest of world:
Osprey Direct UK, P.O. Box 140, Wellingborough, Northants,
NN8 2FA, United Kingdom

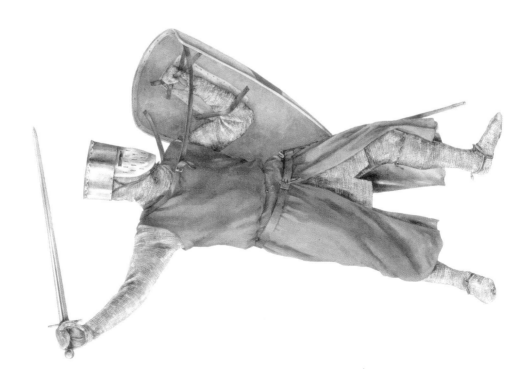

OSPREY
PUBLISHING

www.ospreypublishing.com

call our telephone hotline
for a free information pack

USA & Canada: 1-800-458-0454
UK, Europe and rest of world call:
+44 (0) 1933 443 863

Young Guardsman
Figure taken from *Warrior 22:*
Imperial Guardsman 1799–1815
Published by Osprey
Illustrated by Richard Hook

Knight, c.1190
Figure taken from *Warrior 1: Norman Knight 950 – 1204AD*
Published by Osprey
Illustrated by Christa Hook

POSTCARD